Title page: Liszt's piano transcription of Franz Schubert's song "Die Forelle" [The Trout]. Original edition [Second Version] published by Anton Diabelli & Companie, Paris, 1846. Courtesy of Dr. Rena Charnin Mueller, New York University.

La Danza
and Other Great
Piano Transcriptions

FRANZ LISZT

DOVER PUBLICATIONS, INC.
Mineola, New York

Bibliographical Note

This Dover edition, first published in 2001, is a new compilation of works originally published in authoritative early editions. The poetry paraphrases on pp. vi–vii were prepared specially for this edition.
We are grateful to Dr. Alan Walker for his kind assistance in verifying background information on the works in this volume.

International Standard Book Number: 0-486-41682-8

Manufactured in the United States of America
Dover Publications, Inc., 31 East 2nd Street, Mineola, N.Y. 11501

CONTENTS
Franz Liszt's legendary transcriptions for solo piano
Titles are given in their most familiar form.

Except for the Beethoven and Tchaikovsky transcriptions, all works in this volume were edited by Emil von Sauer.

The Maiden's Wish

Paraphrase of S. Witwicki's poem
Music by Frédéric Chopin (p. 34)

If I could rise into the sky like the sun,
I would eternally hover near your head only—
not around the forests, not around the fields,
only by your window would I hover eternally.

On Wings of Song

Paraphrase of Heinrich Heine's "Auf Flügeln des Gesanges"
Music by Felix Mendelssohn (p. 82)

On wings of song I carry you away, my love—
to fields by the Ganges where I know the most beautiful place.
A garden of red blooms lies there in the soft moonlight . . .
There we will sink down beneath the palm tree,
drinking in love and peace and dreaming a blissful dream.

Elf King

Paraphrase of Johann Wolfgang von Goethe's "Erlkönig"
Music by Franz Schubert (p. 102)

Who is riding so late through night and wind?
It is the father with his child held firmly in his arms;
He grasps him securely, he keeps him warm.
    "My son, why are you hiding your face in such terror?"
       "Father, don't you see the elf king?
       The elf king with his crown and train?"
    "My son, it is a patch of fog . . ."
               ("You dear child, come along with me!
             I will play beautiful games with you . . .")
      "My father, don't you hear what the elf king promises me?"
    "Be calm, my child: the wind is whistling in the dry leaves . . ."

The Trout

Paraphrase of Christian F. D. Schubart's "Die Forelle"
Music by Franz Schubert (p. 110)

In a bright brook the capricious trout
shot by like an arrow in its happy haste . . .
A fisherman with his rod stood watching on the bank . . .
    "As long as the water is clear," I thought,
    "he will never catch that trout . . ."
But he muddied the brook . . . his rod twitched . . .
and I looked at the deceived victim.

Dedication

[Widmung]

Paraphrase of Friedrich Rückert's "Du meine Seele, du mein Herz"
Music by Robert Schumann (p. 130)

You, my soul, you, my heart,
You, my bliss, O you, my pain,
You, my world in which I live . . .
You are repose, you are peace,
You are heaven destined for me . . .
With your love you lift me
    above my limitations,
My guardian spirit, my better self!

La Danza
and Other Great
Piano Transcriptions

Organ Fantasy and Fugue
in G Minor
1863 transcription of the work by Johann Sebastian Bach (BWV 542)

Grave

Ossia:

Fuga

Prelude and Fugue
in A Minor

Transcription, between 1842 and 1850, of the work by Johann Sebastian Bach (BWV 543)

Präludium

Fuga

"Joyous gathering of the peasants"

1837 (revised 1865) transcription of the scherzo from Ludwig van Beethoven's
Symphony No. 6, "Pastorale," Op. 68

2e fois Pédale à chaque mesure

sempre più f

Tempo 1º

The Maiden's Wish

Transcription, between 1847 and 1860, of the song theme, with three new variations,
of Frédéric Chopin's music from *Six Polish Songs*, Op. 74

Waltz from *Faust*

1861 concert paraphrase of music from Charles Gounod's opera

*) Skip to the sign ⊕ , *Presto* [Liszt's note].

Faust: „Ne permettez-vous pas, ma belle demoiselle
Qu'on vous offre le bras, pour aller le chemin?"

Marguerite: „Non, Monsieur, je ne suis demoiselle, ni belle
Et je n'ai pas besoin, qu'on me donne le bras."

*) Skip to the sign on p. 51. *Allegro vivace assai* [Liszt's note]. The cadenza version continues and cannot be cut.

*) See note, p. 50.

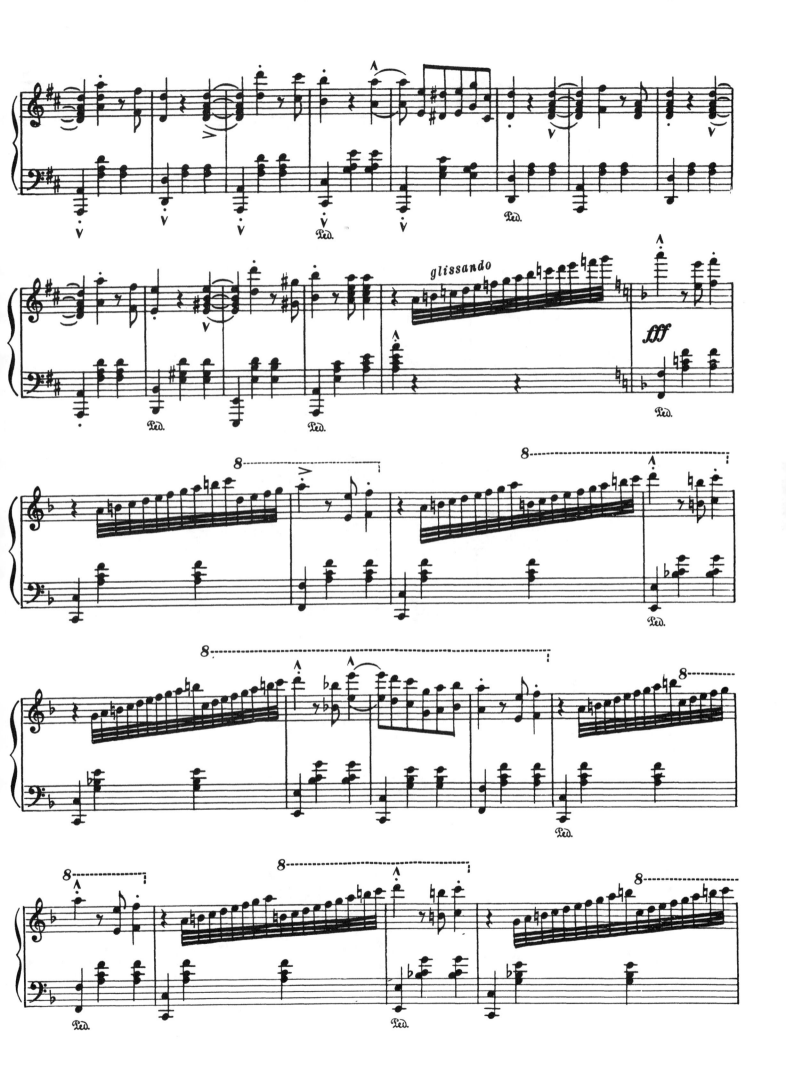

*) Skip to the *Stretta [Presto]* on p. 57. [Liszt's note].

Wedding March
and Dance of the Elves

1849–50 transcription of Felix Mendelssohn's incidental music, Op. 61,
for Shakespeare's play *A Midsummer Night's Dream*

Tempo I Allegro

On Wings of Song

1840 transcription of Felix Mendelssohn's song
"Auf Flügeln des Gesanges," Op. 34, No. 2

Andante tranquillo

*)Die nach unten gestrichenen Noten ♩
mit der linken, die nach oben gestrichenen ♪ mit der rechten Hand

Les notes: ♩ = *main gauche. Les
notes:* ♪ = *main droite*

The ♩ are to be taken by the left,
the ♪ by the right hand

La Danza

Neapolitan tarantella

1837 transcription of "The dance,"
No. 9 of Gioacchino Rossini's *Les soirées musicales*

Presto assai

La Regata Veneziana

Nocturne

1837 transcription of "The Venetian regatta,"
No. 2 of Gioacchino Rossini's *Les soirées musicales*

Erlkönig

1837–8 transcription of Franz Schubert's song "Elf King" (4th version), D328

The Trout

1846 transcription of Franz Schubert's song "Die Forelle" (2nd version), D550

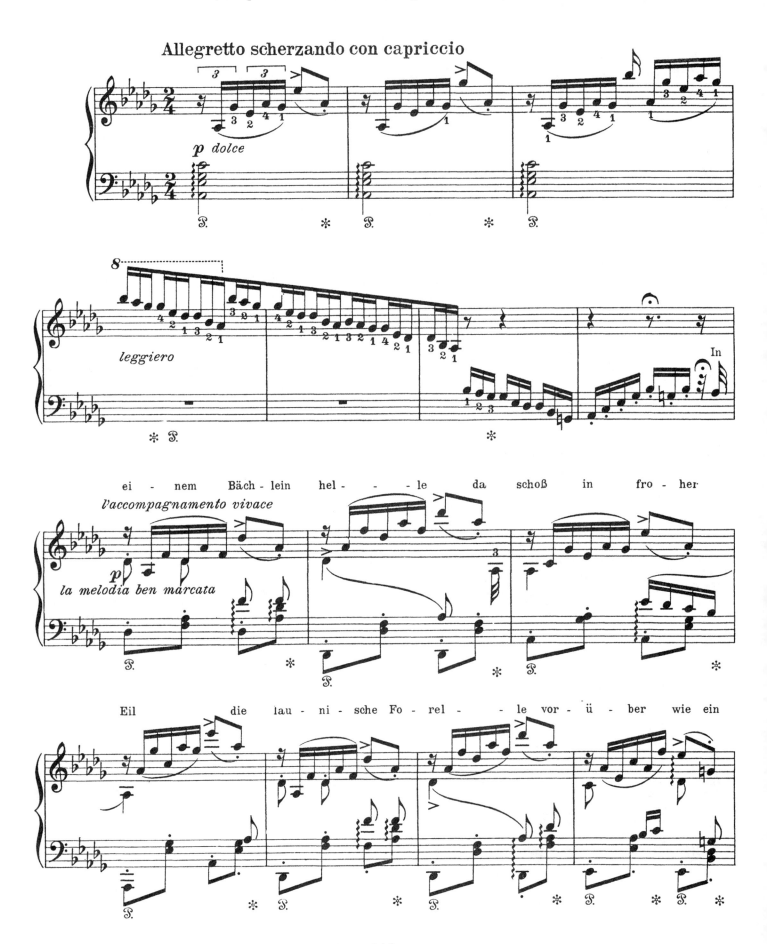

The Trout / 111

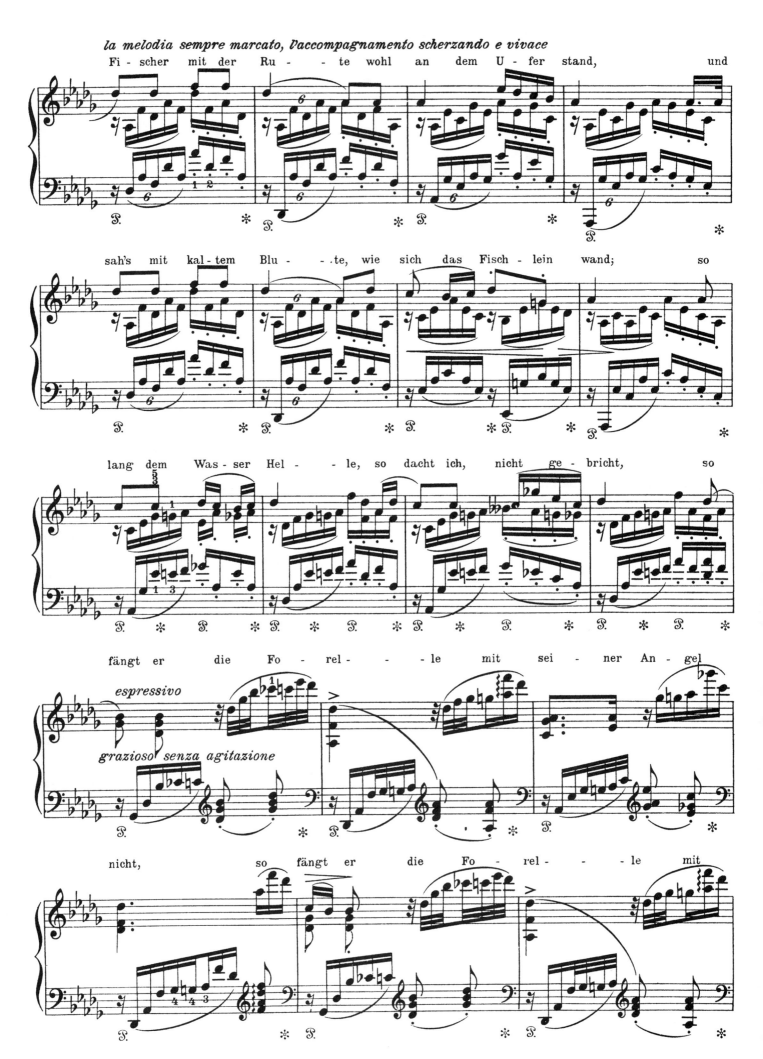

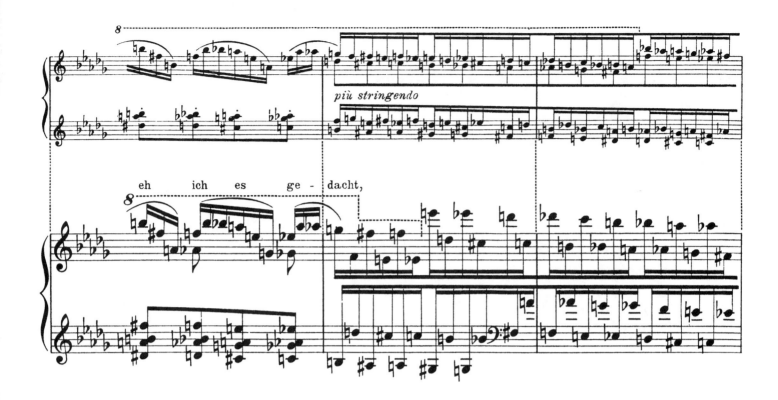

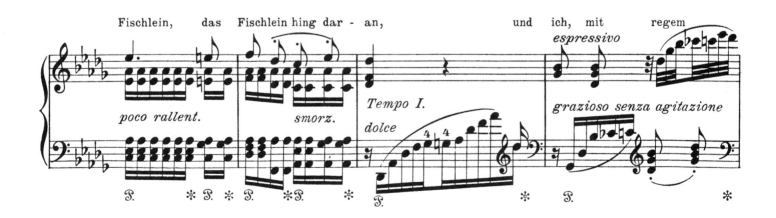

Grand March
in B minor

1846 transcription of the third of Franz Schubert's *Six Grand Marches and Trios* for piano four hands, D819 (Op. 40)

Allegretto fuocoso

Widmung

1848 transcription of Robert Schumann's song "Dedication," Op. 25, No. 1

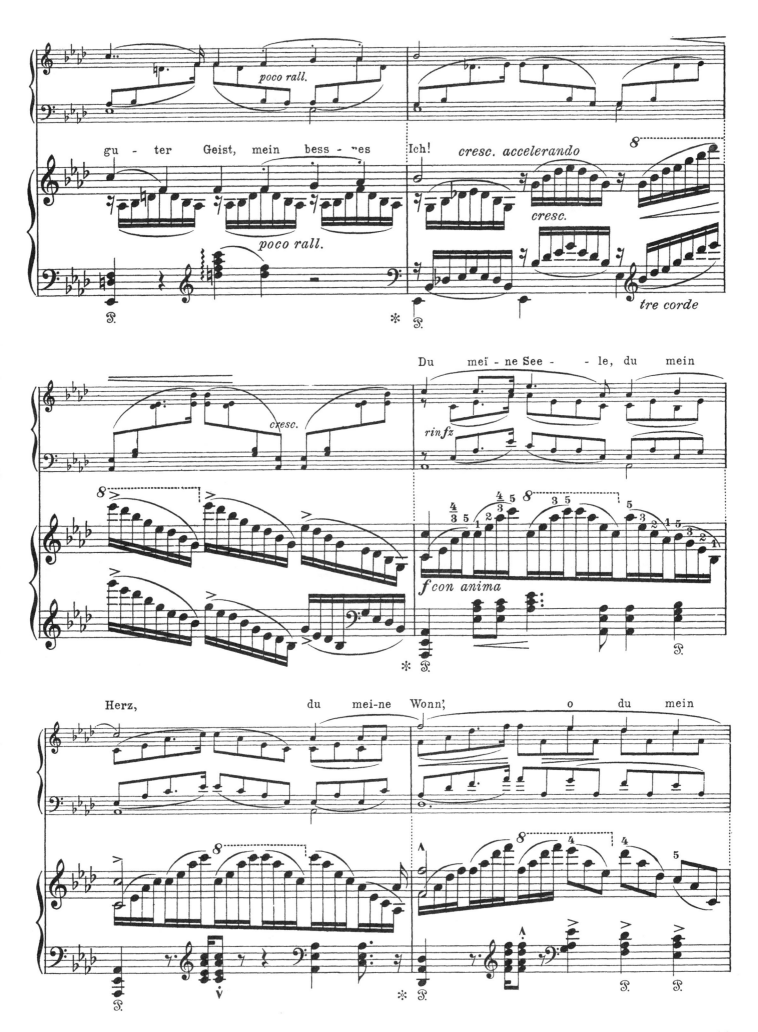

Polonaise

1880 transcription of the Act III ballroom music
from Peter Ilyitch Tchaikovsky's opera *Eugene Onegin*